AGRIDULCE

AGRIDULCE

POETRY AND PROSE

Dhayana Alejandrina

Columbus, Ohio

Agridulce: poetry and prose

Published by Gatekeeper Press
2167 Stringtown Rd, Suite 109
Columbus, OH 43123-2989
www.GatekeeperPress.com

The cover design, interior formatting, typesetting, and editorial work for this book are entirely the product of the author. Gatekeeper Press did not participate in and is not responsible for any aspect of these elements.

ISBN (paperback): 9781662912061
eISBN: 9781662912078

A•gri•dul•ce
Adjetivo

1.

Que tiene mezcla de agrio y de dulce.
Having mixture of sour and sweet.

This poetry book is dedicated to my younger self.
You always knew you wanted to write.
Smile girl, you are doing the damn thing.

Paper is a blank listener
that accompanies me through life.
I can find paper in corners
I could never find you in my heart.
Paper lets me be vulnerable.
It doesn't judge me.
It embraces me for who I am.
As I turn the pages carefully,
paper welcomes me with open arms.
Some of you could never imagine
the relationship that we have.
Paper is a blank listener,
it helps me through my darkest times.

AUTHOR'S NOTE

Writing has always been a part of me. It found me when I had not even found myself. Writing gave me a one-way ticket to a place with no judgment. Growing up in the Dominican Republic, I did not spend much time using technology. Therefore, I mostly focused on school, volleyball, writing, and spending time with my family and friends. Seeing my dad get lost in books, and watching my mom sing so happily, made me eager to have others connect with my words, the same way my parents did with books and music. The truth is, writing makes me feel alive. It is a form of art that gives me the opportunity to entirely express what I feel, and for that, I am grateful.

Agridulce is a combination of emotions, thoughts, and experiences. It is meant to bring awareness to all that we feel as we experience life. Through each flip of a page new content comes to life, so go on at your own risk, because poetry is such a bliss.

INTRODUCTION

This book is divided into two sections: *Lo Agrio* and *Lo Dulce*. The poems and proses in each of these sections are inspired by emotions I have felt, love stories, conversations with people, and experiences that have contributed to my personal growth. I believe that when we create connections with people we tap into different parts of ourselves; learning something new each time. I use poetry to express the journey of human emotions, showing *that to live is to embrace the sweet and the sour in life.*

Lo Agrio

We often suppress negative feelings because we are afraid of others' reactions, or afraid of facing our own darkness. We forget that these emotions can also teach us lessons, reshape our perspectives, and allow us to tap into our most vulnerable selves. As we experience pain, loss, anger and heartache, we are also *experiencing life*. Once we learn to accept these emotions, we will be able to embark on a more meaningful personal journey.

Lo Dulce

At times, pain can come from love, just like love can come from pain. This chapter starts with finding inner peace by experiencing different forms of love—not just a love connection with someone else, but *a love connection with ourselves*. It represents a journey of self-acceptance and healing that leads towards opening ourselves to love, sexuality and self-confidence.

To the Readers

I hope you find a home within my words where you feel safe.

Writing is an art.
A way to express ourselves.
A creativity that we must set free.

LO AGRIO

Can You See Me?

I am covered with scars
the naked eye cannot see;
but I am willing to show
them off for the world
to see me, *for me.*

Heart

My heart hurts
as if someone were
squeezing it to death.
It bleeds slowly,
welcoming pain.
My heart hurts,
but ripping it off?
Not an option.
Feeling it all?
A fatal precaution,
that I must take to stay human.

True Colors

You saw me bleeding,
but instead of helping,
you decided to stab me
while the wound was still open.

A Familiar Feeling

Your voice is the remedy to my broken heart.
It pulls the strings but never breaks it,
like others have.
The sound of your voice I recognize,
like a memory from the past.
Maybe our souls are intertwined
and the universe keeps finding a way for us to reunite.
Perhaps this time you can stay?
Perhaps this time we can last?

Desperate

A desperate heart is willing
to be ripped apart slowly,
to feel anything,
instead of nothing.

Like the Ocean

I am trying not to rush
like the waves rush to shore,
but lately our emotions
have been crashing together.
I find it difficult to believe,
so I ask the ocean to please sing for me,
hoping you will hear its melody.
I am trying not to rush
like the waves rush to shore,
but I am scared that
you no longer hear my voice
as the rip currents take me hostage.
I am trying not to rush
like the waves rush to shore,
but even when I run,
you still feel distant.
I am trying not to rush
like the waves rush to shore,
but maybe the ocean that separates us
is meant to connect us in a way
that we will only understand
once we are drowning in it.

Empty Home

Your voice burns like the flames of hell
as you whisper into my ears words of betrayal.
Our memories flash before my eyes;
I start to feel the distance rise.
Was my love not enough to make you feel at home?
Was my love not strong to hold you through the storm?

Vengeful

Let my words pierce your skin
like a needle piercing clothes.
Trust me, I will not hold back
all the pain that I have felt
through the dark nights.
You put me down—
never picked me up.
Today I hope heavy rains
pour upon your heart,
which does not grow.
Maybe one day, you will learn to love
or the storm will catch you cold,
showing you how life unfolds.

Student of Life

I wish I could tell you that everything is going to be fine,
but if I do, I would be nothing but a hopeless heart
knowing the ending yet choosing to ignore it.

Let Me Be Yours

I want to be the cool picture you take
and stare at, day after day.
I want to be the *"Look at my babe; she's beautiful."*
Of course, I do not need this all the time,
just the times when I feel invisible, little.
Just the times when my hair is messy,
my face is not clear,
or my stretch marks appear.
Those are the times when I need to know
that *you see me.*

It has always been you,
the person I want recognition from.
It has always been you,
the person I want a *"good morning"* from.
It has always been you,
the person I want to hold my hand
as we take a stroll.

I do not need to be displayed like a trophy,
but treat me like the miracle you prayed for,
so much your knees bled.
Please treat me like the last cup of water on a thirsty day.
Please listen to me,
the way a mother listens during a heartbreak.
Please take care of my heart because often, *I can't.*

I just want to be yours.

Disappointed

You lied to me easily,
like the air I breathe.
You had me fooled;
I felt like a clown.
Up and down
like a trampoline,
you had my heart falling for tricks.
Dear love,
you were supposed to bring
happiness and joy.
So, tell me,
where is this pain coming from?

Thoughts on Attachment

The truth is, attachment can become toxic. People misunderstand the law of attraction and think that attachment is a "must" to connect with someone. In fact, you must create deep connections, instead of deep attachments. When you are deeply attached, you become too dependent on the other individual to validate your feelings, thoughts, or worth. You are unable to do it alone, and so you lose power over yourself. When you make deep connections instead of deep attachments, you are still in control of your energy. Creating less attachment allows you to experience life more— welcoming a field of new possibilities.

Coward

Do not start my fire
to leave me burning alone
at the end.

Lost in Thought

Once again, I have found myself in that little spot between nothing and everything; where the answer is clear but the response is imaginary. I am here. No 911 calls to rescue me as I am my own prisoner. I am here. Hoping the walls do not become tighter and the air thicker.

Dhayana Alejandrina

Nostalgic

Wishful of a love
that fills the holes you left in me.
Wishful of a touch so deep,
burning my skin,
inhaling the need
like a drug consuming me.

If a wishing well were close to me
every coin would mean the world to me
every wish would be a dream to me
every second would be a precious treat.

So now and then I hear a voice
whisper through some tiny holes.
Why so nostalgic? says my mind;
I shake my head and close my eyes.
Nostalgia creeps through the night.

*Note: A friend love story inspired this poem
after a rough breakup that left her feeling lost.
A part of her constantly wished for the experience to disappear.*

Living in a Dream

The fairy tales you told me
only proved to be the false
reality you desperately wished to live.
Blinding me with dreams of what could be.
Playing with my emotions
like puppets on your fingertips.

*Los cuentos de hadas que me contaste
solo resultaron ser la falsa realidad
que desesperadamente deseabas vivir.
Cegándome con sueños de lo que podría ser.
Jugando con mis emociones,
como títeres en la punta de tus dedos.*

Over-Thinker

Although I know I am loved,
sometimes *I fear not being loved enough.*

The Thought of You

The night approaches me
whispering into my ears
what it sounds like your name.
I take a deep breath,
remembering the softness of your fingertips
against *my Shea butter skin.*

On nights like these,
when the clouds are vivid
and the wind sings,
I remember you the most.

Fading Away

I am fading,
not captivated,
your love is migrating
as mine stays the same.
I am fading,
like beauty through the years.
As the heavy rain pours
the sound of your voice disappears,
reminding me that the end is near.
I am fading,
my colors infiltrated,
no vivid images
as I fade away.
I am fading,
you left me waiting,
my heart is wrenching,
you are not the same.

A Blind Eye

Let's not pretend our love was an illusion.
For if we do, then we are nothing
but empty vessels refusing to feel;
choosing to live in a world full agony and solitude.

Traumatized

I loved you so much
I forgot to love myself.
To complete you,
I self-destructed as you watched.
Damn, you drained me up.
I remember the days when loving
felt like the first day of summer
after an emotionless winter.
I was a loving soul;
now my heart has pain
as a permanent visitor.
Is this my karma? I asked life.
For being dumb and opening my heart?
What can I do to feel again?
I'm tired of being played.

Libertad

I want to be free
enjoy the air I breathe
no anxiety on sight
just a beautiful starry night

I want to be free
from the demons hunting me
from the pain consuming me
from the walls that are trapping me

I want to be free
from the memories that wake me up
from the tears that taste like salt
and the self-blame that never goes

I want to be free
from what was never apologized for
from the insecurities that say "hello"
from the doubts eating me whole

I want to be free
from the pain that holds my hand
as tight as an oyster

I want to be free,
but my fear drains me
and my lack of self-love scares me

I just want to be free.

Letting Go

I decided to let you go.
We have done so much,
yet so little.
Is life supposed to be this way?
My heart is racing,
jumping like a toad in a thunderstorm.

I decided to let you go.
The cause of death
creeping slowly
as the shadows from the sun.
What a shit show.
My heart is a sucker for love,
a poisonous habit
that welcomes toxicity.

Thoughts on Fear

Fear has the power to consume you to the point of losing yourself and diminishing your value. At the same time, fear is a natural part of life. It can serve as defense mechanism when we have a healthy balance. However, if overly consumed by it, fear becomes a self-destructive tool. Being aware of your worst fears is the first step towards becoming *self-aware;* not doing anything to overcome your fears becomes *self-imprisonment.*

The Bird on Top of the Tree

As I spread my wings,
my body shakes.
>*Is it the beginning?*
>*Or is it the end?*

It is my first jump.

Alive

I am hurting,
but at least I am feeling.
I guess that's part of *being alive.*

Core Memories

I carry your words with me
like a souvenir from the past.

Chances

When you allow
someone to constantly
disappoint you,
your high expectations
become low standards.
How many chances can you give?

First Love

The first time I laid eyes on you
my world went from black and white
to vivid colors, *rainbow-like.*
In a blink of an eye,
I gave my heart to you,
I gave my love to you.
I had no power over my emotions
as I poured them into you.

My first love.

You came into my life like sunshine
then left me in the dark like shadows.
You were everything to me,
but I was only a piece to your puzzle.

Weather Warning

You charmed your aura into my stormy mind
the way lightning marks the sky.
Everything that was clouded cleared up
like the atmosphere clears during the eye of a storm.
That's when you showed me *your true colors*.
Disguised as a rainbow,
yet you were a black hole waiting
to swallow me into infinite solitude.

Homesick

Before wanting to feel at home with someone else,
learn how to feel at home with yourself.

A Message

If my soul could speak
your ears would bleed.

You Were Never Mine

The tide is coming tomorrow and I feel the atmosphere of my body changing. Like a lightning bolt, the idea of seeing you leave strikes my heart with rage. As I stand by the shore, I hear the waves crashing; telling me it is time to let go of what after all, was *never mine*. I shake my head and look at the sky, wondering why I always end up here— *alone, stuck, and vulnerable.*

In the Dark

Late night conversations with my mind
are full of ambiguous thoughts.
I find myself tossing around saying "no"
as soon as pessimistic beliefs try to invade
every inch of me like lava burning
through a harvest I worked so hard to sow.

It is crystal clear to me,
my mind and I have a *love-hate relationship*.

There are nights when she browses
through the archives of my soul
finding pieces of me I thought were gone.
At the same time,
there are other nights when I cannot escape
all the "what if" scenarios
of a life, I have yet to live.
The voices get loud
and I cannot seem to tune them out.

The truth is,
these late-night conversations
help me realize how much power my mind has—
when I failed to *bring myself back to reality*.

Anger

The battlefield is not out there.
You carry it within you
like a ticking time bomb,
waiting for someone to cross you
so you can explode.

Regret

Regret is dwelling
on the minutes
hard to rewind.
Regret is betraying
the present for the past.
Regret is living in doubts
that haunt your mind,
preys on your heart.
Regret blinds you
from the good in life.

Thoughts

Sometimes growth will need *accountability*.
That means facing your truth and acknowledging
your mistakes without making excuses.

Inevitable Truth

I wish
I could *love myself*
as easily as *I love you*.

Here I Am

There were nights when closing my eyes
felt like a death sentence creeping slowly
into every cell of my body
until I could no longer dream.
The thought of waking up
felt more like a threat than a blessing to live.

Still alive, I cling to the meaning of life
hoping I never shift back to the horrible thoughts
that used to consume me at night.
Reflecting into the mirror,
I realize how much I am blessed.
I forgive myself for ever thinking that my existence was
nothing more
than number making up the population count.

As I open my eyes from dreaming all night,
I no longer feel fear sleeping by my side.
I feel free and light
like the clouds drifting through the sky.
My existence does not feel like a burden in my eyes.

I am reborn into my higher self.
I am one with the Earth.
I am one with the Skies.
I am finally, *present*.

Lost

I drifted through your
tasteless sea like an empty
bottle waiting to be found.
Each wave carrying
me farther away
into unknown territories.
From sunrise to sunset,
you played tricks on me
like a master magician.
Hypnotized, I was deceived
by the tip of the iceberg
until I saw the depth of your devilry.

Caught

The idea of letting go of certain memories
hunts me like the moon hunts the sun.
I am caught between the waves of your memory
and deep down, *I want to be taken away.*
Letting go is not as easy as breathing.
Although breathing can suffocate
as you start to overthink.
I am unsure if the memories are slipping away,
or perhaps,
I am.

Needy

I lost sight of the realest part of me.
The part that only becomes visible
when I am *with you*.

Differences

Loving someone is not a sacrifice,
losing yourself to love them, *is*.

Recognition

I do not regret the love I have given anyone in my life.
It was given wholeheartedly and genuinely.
It is theirs to hold tight and find comfort when needed the most.

Blank Pages

A journal is as anguished as the writer.
It has experienced the loss,
felt the hesitation of the pen,
or the wetness from the tears
as they create watercolor stains.

A journal feels,
just as its writer.

Thoughts on Existence

Our souls have their own way of communicating—a *spiritual language* that understands the pain we were born into, and the history behind our fingerprints. There is so much mystery in life, as well as beauty. As we embark into our individual journey, we will discover the power and willingness of our hearts.

Still Hiding

Once upon a time,
I held a secret about myself.
Since my childhood,
it was always there.
Is it unholy to feel this way?
An attraction I cannot understand.

Oh, silly girl, stop that thought!
The Bible says this is ALL wrong!
Oh, silly girl, go back in there!
The closet is now your new best friend.

Anxiety

Mind spins like a spinning wheel
as my thoughts lose reason.
I asked my heart if it can slow down,
I want to keep up but I am in doubt.
Anxiety peeking through,
just saying "hello."
Morning rushing,
my heart is clutching,
and I cannot seem to breathe.
Where is the pause button?
I am in need to rewind life,
find a place of calmness in my heart.

October Ends

Nothing felt more bitter
than the way our lips
parted to say our last goodbyes,
I never thought choking
on words was really a thing
until I saw you walk away
holding every piece of me
within your hands.

Mystery

Life is a mystery.
It gives when you do not ask,
it takes when you need most.
It is like walking blind,
hoping to not step on mines.
Every step you take should be as
precise as the hands of a surgeon,
as delicate as a spiderweb,
as truthful as a knight
fulfilling his duty.

Confessions

I have been treating her like the dirt
under my fingernails.
I have been putting her through hell.
I have been talking to her ugly
and not respecting her beautiful self.
You may think I am a monster
who does not care about her at all.
It has been years since I told her
I was sorry, I was wrong.
There are nights I want to take her
to the mirror and have a talk.
Say "*You are truly magnificent.*
Please hold yourself high."
Yet I stutter like a baby,
turn my back on her again.
Please forgive me for not taking care of you
the way you deserved.

Red Mansion

I ran through the hallways of a mansion
where the walls were all red.
I tried to open the doors
but I was kept away.
I ran and ran in circles.
I had nowhere to sleep.
I was haunted by your memories,
insecurities, and grief.
I tried to feel something
rather than this emptiness inside.
Then I realized,
this mansion in red is nothing but a cold heart
that has never been able to tear down the walls;
the fear of love.

Thoughts on Change

Change is something inevitable. If you do not take *smart risks*, you will not be able to know the true power of your potential. Most people fear change because of the unknown. The fear of leaving behind the comfort zone. The truth is, change will always exist in our personal and professional lives. *We are continuously learning, and adapting.* This is part of change.

Seasonal Love

Please do not let me fall
if you know you cannot catch me.
I refuse to be like autumn leaves,
constantly falling.

Seeds

Heavy to write, heavy to say.
Like many others, I fear birth.
The thought of ever failing you
scares me.
I refuse to transfer you my pain,
the trauma I'm slowly
overcoming every day.
I may not be perfect,
flawed in many ways.
Yet I am eager to one day meet you,
be the mom that you deserve.

Toxic Relationship

I have a toxic relationship with my thoughts
whenever I start to feel alone.
They try to tell me how to feel
and I fall for it,
like bowling pins rolling on the floor.

I have a toxic relationship with my thoughts.
I skip through my memories
searching for something to make me feel present,
but I always end up lost.

I have a toxic relationship with my thoughts
but breaking it would be devastating
as my thoughts are also my shield.
An armor I can never reveal,
a part of me that carries my will.
My memories are who I am
reminding me of who I was
protecting me from falling back
into the habits that once ripped me apart.

Interconnected

In a world full of ache,
we still manage to find
love where we least expect it.
Pain can be born from love.
Love can be born from pain.

Naive

my heart
always ends
up watering
dead seeds.

Embedded

Whether you love me or hate me,
a part of me is engraved within you
like a core memory—
a reminder of my existence.

Dear Driven Girl,

You been so caught up on how your future should be that you no longer see the fruits you birth in the life you currently live. You dismiss little accomplishments as if they mean nothing towards what you wish to accomplish. Driven girl, your experiences have taught you that slowing down is not an option and waiting for others to help causes destruction. I want you to know that living in the moment is something beautiful and an accomplishment. You do not have to slow your roll, but please give yourself some credit for how much you have grown. Remember that what is meant for you will come no matter how fast or slow you go. Celebrate your big accomplishment, but also the small. Every step you take forward is a reflection of your growth, and a genuine helping hand does not always slow your roll.

Survivor

Lost in life,
that's when I met you.
An attraction
became fatal.
Entirely naïve,
I jumped into the flames,
burning along the way.
I started to feel used,
like dirty clothes on the floor,
or unwanted paper
once it is all wrinkled up.

Oh, you thought that was the end?
Let me tell you about the rest.
The manipulation, the threats, the lies.
You made me feel like it was my fault,
you made me want to lose my life.

Waking up was not so easy.
How did I miss the red flags?
Some say, "*You learn the hard way.*"
Trust me, I wish I had never learned this way.

Once free,
I was able to finally breathe—
to see your true colors,
your intentions with me.

Never again will I fall within the hands of someone
who almost took the light away from me.

Dedicated to anyone who has ever felt emotionally,
verbally, or physically abused.

At Last

I was never lying when I said I loved you.
I was just scared my words would go
in an ear out the other.
I know I took a risk
like a bird jumping off for the first time.
I thought giving you a chance was a new start.
Oh, what a thought that was.
When I least expected,
you shattered me into pieces
with so much hatred I could no longer see
the reflection of your soul within mine.
I lost touch with my worth
feeling alone as I lay on the cold floor.
Although whole I am no more,
let me tell you, mi amor;
each piece you pulled apart
allowed me to rebuild into who I truly am.

Pain

It builds you.
It shapes you.
It changes you.
It molds you into who you really are.

Thoughts on Moving On

Moving on means to stop dwelling on the past. It is about understanding the lessons and applying them towards the future you wish to have. Moving forward should not feel like a punishment, but a *necessity to your growth.*

Remember, *healing attracts positive energy.*

Focus on your mind, heart and soul.

LO DULCE

Rebirth

The darkest night
gave birth to the brightest star.

She bloomed in adversity.

Healing

It has been a while
since I felt so much peace.
I will never let it go.

Love Language

What is my love language?
Sometimes I don't know.
I have changed so many times
for people I no longer love.
I used to think
to love is to be the person they want me to be.
I became their life-force,
their double-A batteries.
I satisfied each need,
listened to their request,
filled the holes others left.
I really thought this was OK.

As the years went by,
I did not wait for an apology
to claim my power back.
I found true love within myself.
Each part of me is a realm.

My love language *is me*.
I love myself tremendously,
respectfully,
wholeheartedly.

Deep Connections

Plant some knowledge in me
until I no longer crave anything
but deep conversations with you.
Soulful conversations
over coffee or tea:
Tell me all I want to hear.
Tell me what is your biggest fear?
Let us make connections,
no alterations.
No physical needs,
just two spiritual beings
talking about their dreams.

Acceptance

Accepting ourselves requires that we acknowledge our previous mistakes without letting these mistakes define who we can become. Self-acceptance is a path led by love and humility. We must become comfortable with loving our weaknesses as much as we love our strengths while working every day to become a better version of ourselves. Acceptance is understanding that we are unique in our own way and must not compare our growth with others. Bringing awareness to our behavior, mentality, and personality is an important step towards *self-acceptance*.

I Am

I am transforming my thoughts
into a clear voice.
I am speaking into existence
what I want in this world.
I am taking my power back
and planting my seeds to grow.
I am living gratefully,
blessed to see the sun.
I am *present*.

Resilience

Make sure to thank yourself
for being strong enough to still be here
after all that you have been through.

That matters.

A Conversation with a Flower

Do you see,
that my openness shows the beauty within me?
Like a rainbow up in the sky,
my colors are vivid, *full of life*.
Do you see?
I am alive.
Thus, I grow,
I flourish,
I fall.

Una Mujer Fuerte

Beautiful woman who works hard
with goals in mind
strong at heart.
Been through so much,
could write a book,
yet you decide to live it through.
A wonder woman, you are indeed.
Don't ever doubt your capabilities.

Perseverance

Allowing someone to make me doubt
my spiritual strength would be an insult to myself.
For I have walked through the fire barefoot.
For I have given parts of myself I never got to know.
For I have been lost within myself
then found the light to guide me home.
For I have survived internal battles
I do not wish upon my enemy.

I must hold myself as high as the sky above.
I must never forget where my spiritual strength comes from.

Vulnerable

I have always been beautiful.
I just waited too long to tell it to my reflection.

Breathing

Today it is easier to breathe.
My heart no longer carries
the heavy weights from the past.
I am filling my lungs with kindness,
forgiveness, and sincerity.

Remember

Amid all craziness,
you still built a clear path for yourself.
Through the obscure,
you still shined.
You are strong.
You are beautiful.
You are blooming.

Found Myself

For a while I neglected you.
I stopped giving you
the sun and the water
that you needed to grow.
I hid from you
because you are the only one
who makes me face my fears.
Now I have realized,
you are everything I need,
what makes me feel complete.
The piece I cannot find anywhere else.
Now,
I will never stop putting you first,
loving you first,
taking care of you.
With you I am who I am,
without you
I am nobody.

Safe Place

I want you to dive into my heart
and make the deepest part of me your home.

Pirate Crew

Life has no maps,
yet I follow you like a captain
searching for a hidden treasure—*my heart.*

My first mate
always stands behind me,
reminding me to stay sane,
to not dwell—*my mind.*

My quartermaster
expects me to keep myself held
and not revisit my past after a cup of ale.
How can I do that?
I feel trapped in a battlefield of thoughts
making me doubt my direction and intentions.
Am I in too far to turn around?
Can I keep order and stand my ground?—*my memories.*

My gunner
puts a bullet through my heart,
makes me feel alive—*pain.*

My carpenters,
constantly putting me together
when I am falling apart.
You are everywhere I need you to be.
Without you,
I do not know where I would be— *faith.*

Last are my musicians,
with drums and trumpets.
They chant and sing
reminding me to live.
Onto this blue sea called *life,*
I'll set sail.

Mornings with You

As the sun peeks through the curtains
I see you lying by me, *skin to skin.*
Your eyes open slowly
and a smile forms along your lips.
Is this a dream? you asked.
I shook my head
and giggled.
Then with a gentle touch
caressing my cheekbones,
you said,
"I can't imagine a morning
without the sight of you
to start my day."

Dripping Like Honey

Sweet like honey, *you said*.
Making every inch of me shake.
Pulling my hips close to your face.
I am becoming weaker with every breath.

Quiet Nights

A night where we sit by each other,
appreciating the silence, enjoying the
intimacy that our presence brings to us.

Sexuality

She found me at a really young age.
Opening myself like a fragile book,
I welcomed her.

Little by little,
she showed me that the heart
sees no color, no gender or religion.
Although society had an agenda of its own,
I could not control my emotions
or the curiosity building up.
Can you blame me for that?
For wanting to love whoever I want?

Hello, sexuality, I whispered.

Scared of where my emotions may take me,
I wonder whether I should take off
the mask so the world can see me for who I am.
Would you hold my hand as I take this path?

Sexuality, you have taught me so much.
Even when it hurts
I still find a way to love.
Incredible,
the things the heart can do.

I just want to be somebody's rainbow
when they are feeling blue.
I just want to be the light
that makes them forget about the dark.
I just want to be the reason they no longer hide.

Being Human

We are all fighting our own battles.
We are all learning to let go.
We are all trying to become better.

This is a path that requires *patience, faith and love.*

Thoughts on Human Connections

It is important to appreciate true connections and support one another. Sometimes, simple acts of kindness can go a long way for someone who just needs a moment of your time. It is easy to get caught up with our own issues and pretend they are more important than everyone else's. Spend some time appreciating those who even at their lowest still found the time to lend you a helping hand. I believe that meaningful connections stay during our lifetime—*a strong connection never loses its touch.*

Strength Within You

Each wound has cracks
where the light can still shine through,
reminding us that there is always hope
within our pains.

Alignment

The universe showed her the power of alignment.
She became overwhelmed with gratitude.
A kiss from life placed upon her cheekbone,
thanking her for her resilience during this time

*"The mysterious, yet beautiful way
in which life unfolds is incredible,"* she thought,
embracing every second of it.

Winter Nights

On nights like this
I wish to be wrapped within your arms,
feeling the sound of your heartbeat
as our breaths synchronize.

One Last Time

Let me close my eyes to remember you
before the moon hides to welcome the sun.

Your smile:
Bright like a beam of light.

Your eyes:
The color of fresh honey from the hive.

Your skin:
Soft as rose petals.

Your heart:
Beautiful, gentle, and caring.

Your love:
One of a kind.

Tabula Rasa

It is like the seasons changing
through the year,
planning to keep up with fear.
Anxious to start to a new routine,
but nervous about how it will be.
Would it be good?
Will it be bad?
I take a deep breath,
burying my doubts inside.
I look in the mirror,
a little pep talk.
I know I am ready
for this *fresh start*.

Tell Me Those Tears Are Good

I love when the sound of my voice
reaches places in your heart
my eyes cannot see.
It is almost like the sunlight
as it goes through the clouds
during a warm evening.
Although I want you to say more,
your eyes speak profoundly to my soul:
explaining to me what you cannot with words.

Phone Sex

Your voice,
your tone,
your breathing.
A phone call that wakes
erotic feelings.
A tempo outside my limits.
My fingers feel like a river.
I tilt my head back,
look at the ceiling.
Keep whispering,
I want to hear it.
As you speed up,
I catch my breath.
Should I cum now
or wait for the end?

A Virtue

Be patient,
For even the stars wait
For the perfect night
To shine their light
Upon the sky.

Your time will come.

The Awakening

This is serenity, *she whispered*,
as she walked through the wilderness.
She bears nothing but the fruits
of her accomplishments.

She feels the wetness on her feet,
the softness of the green leaves,
the sun as it kisses her skin.

She breathes in deep,
embracing the present
forgetting the hardship.

Suddenly, she remembers
what it feels to be naked,
spiritually, not physically.
She is in touch with her sixth sense.

Appreciation

I want to thank you for loving me.
I want to thank you for holding me.
I want to thank you for accepting me, not judging me.
I want to thank you for making me laugh.
I want to thank you for guiding me, not pushing me.
I want to thank you for being patient with me.
I want to thank you for never manipulating me.
I want to thank you for holding me accountable.
I want to thank you for reminding me of my worth.
I want to thank you for being honest.
I want to thank you for respecting me.
I want to thank you for being there even when I felt like I had no one.

Negrita

Shea butter baby,
coconut too,
my skin is so brown
it might just turn blue.
Not long ago,
people were rude.
Mulatas,
mulatos,
we were hated, too.

Now I would be a fool
to ever feel disgrace,
about my glow,
my crazy fro,
or this beautiful skin
that turns into gold.

I am a masterpiece of nature,
a rarity birthed by cacao trees.

If you are reading this,
repeat after me,
"My chocolate skin is the best fucking thing."

Inner Self

Once I knew how good it felt *to love myself,*
I could never betray my heart.
I knew my true potential,
the power in my heart.

Dhayana Alejandrina

Comfortable in My Skin

As I stare into the mirror,
I let my fingers run through my curly crown
down the line that separates my lips
and on to my curvy hips.
I close my eyes,
embracing the comfort in my skin
as I fall in love with every inch of me.

Intrigued by the color of my soul,
I dug deeper to discover a realm of self-love.
A world where I am the one in control.
A world where my energy freely flows.

I listen to the sound of heart
as it calls my name;
she has been waiting so long
for me to find myself.

This comfort I feel goes beyond this world.
I own this temple,
it is my home.

Celestial Nights

When the moon met the sun,
it met the other side of itself.
The bright light uncovered the parts that
once lived in the dark,
welcoming curiosity.

When the sun met the moon,
it wished it could spend a night with the stars,
to see the wonders of the night,
to listen to the wishes of a shooting star.

Thoughts on Self

Do not compare yourself to others based on their accomplishments. That is not the way to measure yours, *as we are all going through our own process of growth and acceptance.* What truly matters is the effort you put into what you do every day. You are doing great—keep pushing through. *There are people who believe in you.*

Home

Build a home within yourself
that no one could ever tear apart.
Water the soil and give it love
so the foundation can last.
Put up walls sturdy as iron,
may no one make you doubt your worth.
Decorate the inside with everything
that reminds you of who you are,
and who you will become.
Make this *home* a sanctuary,
where you feel safe and free to feel.
This *home* is yours,
take care of it well
because no one else will.

Speechless

When words are not enough, *I hyperventilate.*
The air in my lungs seems to not stay.
The sound of your voice makes me shake
as my throat dries off like desert rain.

When words are not enough,
I must show you my love
with a heartfelt touch,
a kiss or a hug.

When words are not enough,
I will pull the moon to you
and your beauty will shine
under the midnight sky
breaking the horizon.

A Shower Together

Morning rushing,
heart is pumping,
dirty mirror,
liner smeared.
Turn the water
steamy hot.
Look at me,
then *"rub rub rub."*
Fingertips,
soft and soapy.
Tease me baby,
slide them softly.
Hold on tight,
feel the warmth,
cloudy during shower time.

Heart to Heart

Remember how you
met me in pieces?
I am happy to
tell you that
you have made
me feel whole again.

Thank you.

Medusa

I arm myself with the confidence of a goddess.
I feel no fear as I approach you;
like a snake ready to devour.
My heart is cold,
you fear my desires.

I pin you down—*you moan.*
I am standing my ground,
you are not in control.
I breathe in deep,
your soul I quench.
With every bite I take,
the deeper it gets.

The pleasure increases,
blazing like burning lava.
Then, I stare at you;
becoming weaker and weaker
like the candles melting behind us.

I see you are ready
and I smile, while staring into your eyes.
Then beg you to release,
give all of you to me.

Dhayana Alejandrina

Magia De Tus Dedos

Your fingers caress me softly,
like new guitar strings.
I was tight—
you loosened me up.
Playing tunes
I have never heard before—
you made music out of me.
An overwhelming feeling
I could not repress.
Your fingers found the melody
my body waited so long to sing.

Loyal

Giving all my love to you
is *not a sacrifice*.
You fill me with pure love.
You pick me up from my lowest points.
I am committed to love you,
even when you do not love yourself.

Becoming

From time to time
I must look back at
who I was to remember
who I am becoming.

Patiently Waiting

When God decides to send me blessings,
I will be waiting patiently with my heart as open as a plate.

Journal Entries

I feel calmness within, even though the world constantly spins. I feel like the skies look beautiful on an early rise—giving me a grateful feeling towards life. I feel like each day gives me an opportunity to learn and somehow share my knowledge with others. I feel at ease when I encounter a simple moment or think about a happy memory. I feel happy to have ever made someone feel cared for, loved or valued. *I feel closer to my dreams*. I feel thankful for those who ever made me smile after crying. That is how I feel today.

April 2, 2020

Mother Nature

The forest,
unique scenery,
roots deep down,
nature sounds all around.

The forest,
powerful creation,
with a strong foundation,
conveying beautiful symmetry.

An Old Soul

I have lived through many life times.
I have seen countless twilights.
I have been broken-hearted,
tossed to the side like garbage.
I have also been in love;
with the flowers as they grow,
with the beauty of the unknown,
with myself as I evolved.

You can call me *an old soul*;
a traveler of the world,
a shapeshifter from beyond,
or a star as you look up.

First Performance

Hasty breathing,
uncontrollable nerves.
The music is appealing,
yet my heart is screaming.
Word for word
I memorized each line,
even the spaces where the ink smeared dry.
Natural look,
simple is best.
All eyes on me,
I take a deep breath.
I've never performed in front of a crowd
so please be gentle when you make a sound.
Allow me to teach you a thing or two.
Allow my poetry to speak to you.

Men Want Love Too

Men want love too,
the same way women do.
It may be hard to notice
as their thick layers
do not allow vulnerability to show.
Their instincts get in the way,
and emotions become *prey*.
Their minds tell them loving is a weakness
that would take away their strength
becoming weaklings instead.
Although they crave love,
I wonder how long they will put up a front?
Behind all the layers
lies a heart the ocean cannot measure.

Dear men who want to be loved,
let me love you like the ocean loves the coast,
with an abundance of care that nourishes the soul
and never leaves you waiting when you need water to grow.

You

In a world full of broken hearts,
you are the person who gives me life.
The only one whose name means more
than simple letters colliding as one.

To Feel Loved

On nights like these
I wish for a goodnight kiss,
a soft touch against my skin,
a sweet smile as I start to dream.

Dear Moon,

On days like these, I wonder if you feel alone?
When the stars disappear through the night
and your reflection can only be seen in the ocean—
yet, no ocean is in sight.
I wonder if you miss the other half of yourself
as you slowly fade away to welcome the sun.
At least you still have the company of your thoughts
when the sky is empty.
Or is it empty?
I guess it is a matter of perspective;
like whether someone sees the glass half empty or half full.

Dear Moon,

I wonder how it feels to admire other constellations at night
as they paint the atmospheres with their beautiful presence.
I see it now, you are never truly alone—
for you are one with the universe and its energy.

Thoughts on Letting Go

There will be people in your life who do not deserve your time, energy or love. They may test you or even hurt you in the most undesirable ways just to feed their pride and hide their fears. No matter how much you care or tell yourself that you love them, *your well-being,* in its entirety, *matters the mos*t. Leaving behind what does not bring you peace, happiness and growth is not selfish; *it is self-love and self-respect.*

A Writer

A writer is raw, unfiltered.

Picking up a pencil or typing from a phone,
a writer gives life to the emotions you're scared of the most.
Never ashamed of what's inside,
a writer lets the words be born from the heart,
giving you chills as you read from left to right.

A writer is brave, alive and present.

Island Girl

No electricity to charge my body,
only sunshine from the forest.
Coconuts and sandy feet,
I grew up where I was free.
Island life,
no snow in sight,
dark outside,
the moonlight shines.
Island girl
born and raised,
catch me under heavy waves.

Self-Reminder

I see the cracks and the sharp edges.
Yet, I still think you are incredibly beautiful.

Little Things

I'm not the one who wants the luxuries.
I just want the little things.

For example:

Remind me of the time we met
or when we first made love.
Hold my hand in public,
let them know I'm yours.
Place a kiss upon my forehead
as I am waking up.
Bring me back to reality,
when I drift into the unknown.
Leave me a sticky note on the fridge
after a long school night.
Give me M&Ms and Boba
when I'm moody, stressed or sad.

Let's go for nature walks,
laugh at people we don't know.
Let's get some sushi,
talk about our dreams and goals.

I'm not the one who wants the luxuries.
I am just the little things.

Deseandote

Making love to you
is an indescribable feeling
that overwhelms my body,
tensing my muscles
as I cling to you.
Our desires emerging,
spreading through the roof.
As you grab my neck closer to your lips
I see the fire in your eyes,
how deep you feel inside.
Your heartbeat synchronizing with mine
as we make love under the moonlight.

Peaceful Love

Everything was so loud
inside my head
until you finally *whispered*
into my heart.

My Skin

I am shedding the skin you left me in.
I am no longer dry or cracked from within.
Each stage of this transformation
is the evolution of myself.
I am releasing the trauma I held so tight,
I am becoming a woman of light.
I embrace this moment of change
and look at myself with so much strength.
This new skin will shine so bright
the sun will have to cover his eyes.

Susquehanna Days

I still remember our first kiss.
We were texting the night before—
you made me feel like I could never resist
your hands pulling me closer to your skin.
I still remember our first kiss.
The anticipation took over me
with a feeling of excitement
that made me shake instantly.
I still remember our first kiss.
You were blocking the door
at the end of English class—then the bells rang.
It is now or never, I thought to myself
as I brushed away
every bit of self-doubt, shame or regret.
I still remember our first kiss.
You looked so shocked;
you did not move.
Your lips felt full, soft, smooth.
I still remember our first kiss.

The Real Me

I'm not trying to compete with others,
I'm just trying to break generational curses.
To set an example for the ones to come.
To feel happy with my decisions,
never doubting if they were right or wrong.
To look back and see the growth,
never wishing I had more.
To be proud of who I am
knowing that I have always tried.
I'm not trying to compete with others,
I am only competing with myself.
I come from nothing materialistic.
Therefore,
I know how to appreciate
the *wealth of nature and life.*
Like the fresh air as the ocean waves crash.
Like the moments of silence.
Like early mornings welcoming the sun.
I'm not trying to compete with others,
I just want to be the best version of myself.

Mirror into My Soul

A glance in the mirror is a dive into the soul.
A soul groped by the stones she once built up.
A buildup of heartache,
resentment, sadness, regret and guilt.
Guilt that drives disappointment,
heartache that haunts her by sunset.
But a sculptor resides in her consciousness;
a consciousness that ignores her potential.
She grabbed that point chisel and sculpted
the stone pieces embracing herself.
Carved out the weight and joined the old
pain with her new self.
She then remembered that through
pressure and stress a beautiful gem
she becomes: *a diamond soul.*

Reincarnating as a Bird

Early mornings are the best
as I sing with the other birds
welcoming the sun into a new day.
I spread my wings
as wide as the Earth underneath,
then let the wind guide me
towards my destiny.
I am reborn to who I am—
a free soul in the big blue sky.

Women Around the World

You are a blessing sent from God,
no matter what the world seems to tell you.
You wake up every morning one of a kind
and no one should ever take that away from you.
You glow in ways only the sun recognizes
and your growth is majestic.
You are a woman of courage and many strengths.
You are caring, vulnerable, kind, nurturing and life-giving,
but you are also strong, fearless, and could shake the Earth
itself for your voice to be heard.
No matter what life throws at you,
you hold your ground and stand tall.
I admire you.
You are beautiful,
you are becoming.

Strength

Your strength goes
further than the naked eye can see.
Your strength is so vivid,
gray colors turn green.
Unpolished.
Untamed.
Never caged away.
Your strength goes beyond
any mountain ranges.
Your strength is like waters
erupting with flames.
Your strength is the reason
you wake every day.

Proud

Proud to see another day
coping with my mistakes
arriving at a better place
I am proud.
Proud of the woman I am becoming
overcoming great obstacles
I never thought were coming
I am proud.
Proud of my surroundings
living in the moment
makes me feel grounded
I am proud.
Proud of my accomplishments,
in this world of uncertainty
where the urgency is to grow
I am proud.
Thankful for my family
driven and humble
loving and caring
I am proud.
Proud of being truthful
useful
neutral
with my decisions
I am proud.

Family

The roots go so deep I can hardly believe
I am part of this family.
I have never felt such a strong bond
much wider than the world—
this is family.
When I feel like there is no escape
like my life is fading away
I know my family will be there—
that is family.
When the lights turn dim
and the directions you cannot read,
believe deeply in your soul
family will be there to guide you home—
that is family.
When others see nothing
they see you whole;
when you feel defeat
they plant hope—
this is family.

Agridulce

You are *sweet* on the outside;
your looks,
your words,
your expressions,
look invitingly *sweet*.
However, once I got to know you
I saw the melting parts of your skin,
the *bitterness* that comes from within.
I learned that your *sweetness* can be a lust,
just temporary tease.
The *sweet* part of you was only a mask
to cover the *sourness* inside.

Thank You

Thank you for swiping
or for flipping each page carefully.
Thank you for taking the time to stay with me.
Thank you for being vulnerable and carefree.
Thank you for opening your heart to poetry.
Thank you for giving me a chance to write
as I needed to let go of what is felt inside.
Thank you to those who let me share
a piece of their experiences here and there.
Thank you for smiling, laughing, or crying.
Poetry has that power.
Just do not forget to feel it all:
the pain,
the sadness,
the happiness,
the joy.
There is no existence without them all.
Thank you for staying until the end.
Thank you for giving me this chance.

ABOUT THE WRITER

Dhayana Alejandrina is a Dominican writer and poet. She started to write short poems around the age of nine when she lived in the Dominican Republic. She used to write all over her bedroom walls and draw. When she was a child, her parents always encouraged her to follow her artistic side and be proud of everything she created. At the age of 13, in 2009, she moved to the United States with her family. She did not speak English but was able to learn it in a year and a half. She continued to write in her journal, but it wasn't until August 2018 that she first started to share her poetry online. Besides her focusing on writing, Dhayana holds a Bachelor's Degree in Business Administration with a Spanish minor and a Master's Degree in Human Resource Management. Dhayana considers herself a very dedicated and passionate individual who uses writing to connect with others and show the world that it is important to embrace all types of emotions.

*"Writing is a form of love, a form of expression,
a way to capture life."*

Dhayana sees her work as a representation of herself and the world around her. Most of her work revolves around the idea of "owning our emotions and learning to heal through acceptance." She explores different topics such as growth, love, loss, sexuality and spirituality. At the age of 19, she had her first spoken-word performance at a small lyrical lounge in Okinawa, Japan. After that, she fell in love with her potential as a writer and performer. She has participated in several online spoken-word performances, and had her poems featured in the anthology *Soul Candy* by Writer's Pocket, in Issue 5 of the international magazine *PottedPurple,* as well as The Dominican Writers Collective Newsletter for Women's History Month. Dhayana is working on her second book, which is a collection of poems representing the beginning of her writing journey. She hopes to continue her passion for poetry and connect with others through her words.

ACKNOWLEDGMENTS

First, I want to thank God for keeping me healthy and allowing this dream to become a reality. I dreamt of this day for years, and here we are. As a little girl, I fell in love with poetry and the freedom that writing gives me. I believe that words are powerful and can have a huge impact on the people around us. I used to watch my dad read and write a lot. He would always write me a poem on my birthday and would fill journals with creative writing. Growing up in the Dominican Republic I never thought I would be a writer. I have played volleyball since I was five years old and was involved in a lot of school activities—yet, I never knew I would fall in love with writing the way I have. In my 25 years of life, I have been through a lot. The moments that I once thought I could never overcome have made me stronger than before. I am eager to keep experiencing life while expressing myself through writing. I want to thank God for blessing me with this gift.

"Writing can help heal the soul and unwind the mind.
Writing is such a beautiful art."

Secondly, I want to thank my husband Lamont, my family, and my friends for always being supportive, and encouraging me to believe in my craft. There were days when I felt like my writings were not good enough. Days when I doubted my capabilities and wanted to give up. Those were the days when the closest people in my life lifted me up and reminded me how much of a badass I am. My heart is full to be surrounded by an amazing support system. I want you all to know that I am thankful and grateful for you. Thank you to those who read over my poems, told me they were proud of me, or constantly asked me when was the book coming out. I appreciate you and love you. Thank you for always being great.

In addition, I would like to thank Victoria Helena (@victoriahelenaart) for creating the illustrations and cover art for this book. You are extremely talented. I can't wait to see your beautiful art all around.

Lastly, I want to thank the entire Gatekeeper Press publishing team for creating a trusting environment for me as a new author and caring about the quality of my book. To my Author Manager, Nicole Dudley, thank you for always being prompt and willing to answer my questions. You always ensured that I felt comfortable throughout this process. To my editors, Karen K. Craigo and Jason Pettus, thank you for giving me honest and meaningful feedback on my writing. I appreciate that. Thank you so much, GPP Team!